Sally is the first accountant I've ever met who can cut across the jargon and help business owners understand how to take control of their financial and business futures. This book is like a breathe of fresh air.

It is supportive and empowering. It should be recommended reading for any small/medium business owner that wants to thrive.

Aime Ayrehart
Ninja HR
HR & Workers Trade Union

The practical nature of 'No BS Guide to Business Planning' by Sally Brady alongside the somewhat 'frank' vocabulary and not so 'grey suit' humour will get you not only writing your business plan but wanting to write your plan.

Then you'll be hooked and will be twisting and turning that plan to suit you; afterall you are the most important employee, aren't you? And, if being the most important employee isn't what you were expecting, then you better ready yourself for a hug from Sally for managing your cash!

Julie Davis, *Ryedale Group*

If you are looking for a straight-talking business planning book with zero BS, then this is the one for you. Sally says it as it is!"

Nick Inge
Chief Executive Officer
itrust assurance

If you are business owner, start-up or anything in between then you need this book. Sally's straight talking no BS approach encompasses every part of business you need to know about in order to make your profit not only sustainable but trackable too.

It is not overcomplicated with over the top glamorous quirky quotes, it is straight-talking laced in the direct humour that makes this book human and realistic. If you don't read this book because you think it might be boring then I have two words for you... B*** S***!

I am very proud of you and think what you have written is something you should hold as an achievement, you can do this SB and I always knew you could.

Georgia Brady
Digital Marketing

Sallys approach to finances and cashflow is simple, jargon free and cut's past all the "bullshit" as she would say. Her passion for helping people is abundantly clear when reading this book which has been laid out so simply and methodically. If you follow her steps (like I have) you will have a profitable business that keeps paying back year on year which means you get to live the life you want without the burden of the worry.

Highly re

The No B*** S*** Guide to Business Planning

Not Another Boring Business Book

**I show you how to improve
your financial knowledge to create
sustainable profit & growth.**

SALLY BRADY

www.purplestarpublishing.co.uk

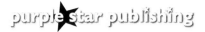

First published in Great Britain 2023 by Purple Star Publishing

Design by Clare McCabe www.purplestardesign.co.uk

ISBN13: 9798395024602

Dedication

This book is something I really never envisaged on my life path and I certainly could not have achieved it without the support of my family and friends. As with any good speech I will have missed someone out or offended someone, but heyho tough shit you should know me by now!!

Firstly to Georgia, aka G, my biggest achievement in life, my biggest supporter – thank you for patience and support in writing this and being part of the journey, I love you with all my heart (I do have one!!), for also being not only my daughter but my business partner too.

My sister Julie for resisting the temptation to edit whilst reading the draft copy!

My Mum and Dad (Eric and Patricia) you made this all possible with your never-ending support.

Clare McCabe you made this happen!

Ash Lawrence and Nick Inge you knew before I did that this was already possible.

Paul Astley for making me smile my way through all the photographs.

To you lot reading this book, a huge thank you for your support.

Contents

Foreword

Ash Lawrence
The FlipFlopPsycho

I was first introduced to Sally Brady by another member of the Chamber of Commerce in August 2020. Sally wanted to come along to one of our ABC Networks meetings and after speaking to her I quickly realised that she would be a valuable member of the group.

Very soon after her joining our network group my instincts were absolutely right and she soon became one of our group leaders and highly respected among our members.

Moving on Sally soon became a client of mine and my preferred person to refer into my clients as the cashflow expert. I believe that what gets measured gets managed and most small businesses are rubbish at doing this. Sally is the perfect person to help them do exactly that; measure it and manage it.

This book has loads of really great tips and is delivered exactly as Sally is, direct and no bullshit (I can't think of anyone else like that?) She knows WTF she is talking about and If you work through the book you will have all of the tools you need to prevent you from becoming a statistic in the failed business list.

One thing though, reading and learning it is not enough, you must implement what you learn. I promise you this much, if you do apply it you'll never worry about money again.

Sally not only teaches this stuff she applies it in her own business and that is one of the main reasons that she has been so successful. My clients love and appreciate her, Sally's clients love and appreciate her and you will love and appreciate her book. Stop mucking about and Do It Now!

Sally Brady

Introduction

Who Am I?

Good question, one I often wonder about too. I'll endeavour to solve this quandary with a brief but definitely not boring overview of my heritage and career and why I'm sat writing this not-so-boring business book today.

> I am Sally Brady, author of this "Best selling Guide to Business Planning" – it had better bloody well be as there's a lot of blood, expletives and sweat gone into writing it!

I started life in the depths of East Yorkshire/Humberside at a time when this part of the world was battling with its identity, wanting to be Yorkshire but with the local government's finest deciding it was a part of Humberside. Needless to say, they were beaten into submission, and we proudly became East Yorkshire again. Anyway, I digress...

I had no idea what I wanted to do with my life upon leaving school. I was a mediocre student more attuned to English and Geography than Maths, so, as with most kids, I fell into my first job, selling wooden boards to building firms. Yep, I hated it, but it paid me £25 a week so it kept me in partying for a while.

During my time in my first job, I started talking to the firm's Accountant and I was given a few bits of bookkeeping to do and found I quite liked it. Despite being mediocre at Maths, I found my path.

You see, much as Accountants - aka the grey suit brigade - want you to believe it's a difficult job and only a Maths genius can attempt the work, Bookkeeping and Accounting are actually more about logic than Maths.

I carried on along the bookkeeping path and I found another job where the firm's Accountant took me under her wing and nurtured my love of Accounting. I went to college one day a week and then had a go at my CIMA exams, not finishing the exams though, due to the

arrival of the finest achievement of my life – my daughter.

However, I kept progressing up the ladder despite not finishing my exams, and found I had a thirst for knowledge around Accounting and Taxation and was like the proverbial sponge, soaking up every bit of knowledge I could.

Despite my lack of final qualifications, I had a damn good career. Working for some serious players in the corporate world, with the experience and knowledge I gained - i.e., my qualification by experience - I could wipe the floor, and still do, with many of the "qualified Accountants" I know today. Whilst I respect a qualification, I have little respect for those who have never stepped into the commercial world and experienced the practicality of running a business and are only theorists who cannot practise what they preach.

Hence I explain in this book that you do not need to be an Accountant or mathematician to understand the Financials of your business.

My corporate career came to an end in 2018. I was frazzled and tired of being beaten by unrealistic profit targets, squeezed in terms of my team resource, and after attending a workshop in Belgium, decided that what I had learnt, and with my years and years of experience, I could go it alone. My friends and family had been saying for years, "Why don't you set up in business on your own? You'd be good at it!" Actually, I think most of that was, "Will you do my personal tax return?"

> No I bloody won't! I hate personal
> tax – use a grey suit!

Sorry, digressing again...

So, at the start of 2018, I began a coaching qualification as I wanted to help people like myself who had been beaten up by the corporate world, and whilst this would be another string to my bow, I found myself falling back to what I love most: Business and Accounting.

I did my research and built my plan and my niche, which actually came easier than you'd think! The one thing I'd had a huge amount of training in while working for big companies was Business Planning and Forecasting, and Cash Management of course. The companies I had worked for were always shit hot in these areas and left nothing to chance and I saw the impact this could have on small - to medium-sized businesses.

I could offer them the knowledge and tools that the big corporates have, but without having to have the big team around them – six simple steps to help people like you to plan and be profitable.

> *And so*
> **Sally Brady, Business Planning Specialist**
> *was born!*

However, March 2020 and COVID hit, bang right at the start of my great plan. All around me, businesses were "pivoting". That damn word should be removed from the English Dictionary. Every coach in the land was using it to guide people. It was absolute bollocks. It showed exactly what I was starting to build my business around: PLANNING. If half the businesses that failed had only had the knowledge on Cash Management and Forecasting and a clear Business Plan, they may have survived.

They would have been able to have the vision or foresight to use the grants and loans wisely and manage their way out of COVID. Instead, we saw business after business fold through lack of cash and huge borrowing that they just could not manage.

During the pandemic, I ensured I stuck to my plan and measured every step of the way. My cash forecasting was also key as I had to be careful with my money and ensure the business could support both itself and me, and sure enough it did. My first year was tough, but I followed the steps I teach on my **Business Planning 101** course (which you will discover in this book) and we had a decent turnover and profit, despite the opening and shutting of businesses during that time.

As the years have gone on, I have continued to practise what I preach and the business has grown every year, so much so that I hit my capacity and am proud to say was able to offer my daughter her first role in business! She too is now following the **BP101** course and setting up her own arm of the business, so you see, what I teach works, or in my own words:

> This Shit Works!

My driver to write this book is just to show you that by having a plan and clear visibility of your numbers, your "Financials", you too can have a business built on sustainable profit and not be afraid of the Financials of the business.

They are the key to profit.

Follow the steps in this book, and even join us on the **Business Planning 101** course and we will show you what a difference it can make to your journey in business: start on the right track or get back on track, whichever it is for you. This book shows you six simple steps to profit.

And as a special thank you for buying my book, and to find out if you are ready to plan for profit, sign up for my free book bonus here: https://tinyurl.com/2p87nvcx. Or get in touch with your Business Planning questions: sally@sallybrady.co.uk

Sally x

Chapter 1

What is a Business Plan and Why Do I Need One?

In simple terms, a Business Plan is a documented map of the goals of your business, it defines your plan for a profitable business.

Many businesses when they start, assume that after a year or so they'll make a profit, but with no defined road map of how to get there, it's on a wing and a prayer. Some get lucky, some don't. More often they don't and it's because they have no structure or plan to work to, no visibility from the start, and no goals to mark their achievements.

There's an age-old notion about it being acceptable not to make a profit in the first two years in business so that you avoid paying tax. That's the first bullshit myth statement of many I will dispel for you in this book.

To me, that's one of the many "bad business owner" statements.

> *You are in business to make a profit and a result of that profit is, wherever you are in the world, that you'll pay tax – end of!*

Do not make this a prerequisite for your business at the start, middle or end!

Now, let's address "goals". I often hear people scoff at the term, but I think that's more out of a lack of understanding of how you can use them to drive you, both in life and business. I don't believe in setting the goal or bar so high it's unachievable; it's about setting yourself something realistic and achievable that you can celebrate along the way, something that by hitting each one, will move you and your business forward.

You can call them "targets" if you don't want to use the term "goals", but what I will say is whatever term you use, put the goals and targets in place from Day One to move yourself forward, or if you're already in business, then start implementing these now to give you more focus. Not having this focus, you'll end up on the hamster wheel, always wondering where you are and when to get off.

The Business Plan map consists of several elements that give you full visibility of your business journey over a period of time. Most businesses I work with look at the next 1 to 3 years, but you may want to go beyond this and have a complete plan for 5 or even 10 years, including either an exit scenario or to sell your business. It is your choice regarding the time span, my advice would always be to pick at least 1 to 3 years. One is not enough – by the time you've started, the year is over; two gives you some focus, and three gives you a clear goal for growth. Anything beyond that is ambitious – possible but ambitious – and will give you more unknowns, particularly when the economy is unpredictable, which is an "always" as opposed to a "sometimes" scenario.

I always look at the length of the plan in clearly defined scenarios. It can be:

- The Start of the Road

- The Middle of the Road

- The Exit Plan

So, think clearly about where you are and which one of these you are building. If you are a start-up, this is easy: you are at the "Start of the Road". If you're in business already and have been for more than two years, you are looking at the "middle" or "exit" scenarios.

Why Do You need a Business Plan?

> It's simple if you want to succeed and have a strong profitable business that has the foresight for sustainable growth, then you need to plan it, not wing it.

Successful businesses are ones that keep up with change and evolve over time. Even during tough times, they have the visibility to adapt, be agile and grow profits, and they do this with a plan and strategy for growth. They will revisit their plans and forecasts monthly, quarterly and annually, challenging themselves further and adapting the plan to become more ambitious.

Business plans give you structure to build a profitable business, enable you to manage cash more efficiently and give you that end goal to work towards. I cannot put it any simpler than this.

I have met many successful business owners who tell me they never had a Business Plan, but the more I talk to them and the more they tell me, I hear about a target they wanted to reach. They tell me how they achieved it, and how they grew the business and what elements they put in place, when they employed staff and how it came to fruition – and the more they talk, the more they realise they did have a plan, so that "bravado" of not having a plan was another one of those "bullshit myths" I dispel for you: successful businesses always have a goal: PROFIT - and how they do it is by PLANNING.

I for one would not be writing this book today if I had not planned my business and not worked with other businesses who wanted and needed to plan for profit in their business. I'd be writing a children's book instead, (although I'm not sure I'd be any good at that; my daughter will tell you my "parenting skills" have been somewhat questionable over the years as I've dragged her to so many business events, it probably would still have been some boring book about business.)

This chapter is short as there is no point me waffling on about how Business Planning can help you plan for sustainable profit and growth and the visibility it gives you over and over again.

> It really is that simple it gives you a clear roadmap to profit, it's the Google or Apple Maps of planning for profit, and stops you going off-piste on a shitty, bumpy, potholed road into losses, and ultimately losing your way and your business.

All I need to add is crack on through the book and soak up everything I'm showing and sharing with you. This book covers each of the things you need to build a solid Business Plan, so get cracking and let me know how you get on. Don't forget, I'm all over Social Media or mail me at: sally@sallybrady.co.uk.

Recap:

1. **What is a Business Plan?**

   It's a documented map of the goals of your business, it defines your plan for a profitable business.

2. **Why do I need a BP?**

   To have a strong profitable business that can grow and evolve with a clear direction.

Chapter 2

Why DO Small Businesses Fail?

I'm sure you've all come across the statistic that 95% of small businesses fail within their first five years, along with the whys and wherefores, the lack of cash, poor marketing, lack of sales, lack of planning that led to that failure. All of which are true, but what REALLY is it, what makes so many businesses fail so quickly?

There are many theories and conflicting views here. Some say it's about not knowing how to sell; some say it's little or poor marketing and expecting sales to just happen. Generally, these are the two main ones people point to.

Over the last few years, I've seen two main sticking points that continually crop up with business owners and entrepreneurs I've worked with, not only on my **Business Planning 101** course but as 1:1 clients too.

Firstly there is FEAR/RESPECT for money.

> Secondly, it's the lack of direction and understanding of the DREAM.

both of which are huge factors that impact small business owners. If you get these right from the start, it will prevent you from becoming another statistic, another notch on the bedpost of failure.

So, whilst the theories and statistics are on point with the facts and figures, for me it's the mindset of the business owner that is the ultimate winner or loser, and the deciding factor of whether you are likely to still be in business beyond the five-year mark.

So, what are the FEAR/RESPECT for money and the DREAM about, and why are they so important for you and your business? I'll explain...

FEAR and RESPECT for Money

What I'm talking about here is, very simply, if you have a bad relationship with money personally then it'll flow naturally into your business. I can hear you saying "Rubbish, it's different." Actually it's not, if you can't be bothered to track your money in your personal life, why would you do it for your business? If you spend without thinking in your personal life, then again you'll be the same in business.

Cash, or lack of it, is the main killer in business.

> Tight Cashflow creates desperation, and desperation smells like "dog shit"

(my own business coach says that time and time again!) It repels people from buying from you and you start to make poor decisions that impact the wellbeing of your business and, hey ho, that's you down the Swanny before you even blink!!

Depending on how you've been brought up as a child, and how money affected you then, this is a factor that will also impact how you treat money in your adult life, and ultimately, your business. Do you respect money? Does it ebb and flow in your life? Are you a saver, or are you a scrimper?

All these points impact how you run your business. If you can respect money and make it work for you, then you're onto a winner. You may think you grew up fine and never had to worry about money, or you may have promised yourself you wouldn't be like your parents, and you would always ensure that you had money. But look over your life now and your money patterns and ask yourself,

"Do I respect my money?"

You have to get this part right and get your head around it now. Even if you've already started your business and you're a few years down the road, I can guarantee there are a few mistakes and won't-do-that-again scenarios and stories you'll have. You may even be on the hamster wheel of debt.

Don't get me wrong – there are times when you need to borrow to advance your business, or even start it, but – and a huge BUT – if you haven't got the money relationship right, I'm damn sure you'll be making one or two of those mistakes again, and that hamster wheel may even become a never-ending cycle until you fall off and fail.

So, take a deep breath and be honest with yourself: what is your relationship with money really like? Don't kid yourself, or cheat, as it's only you you're cheating. Your success depends on your honesty with yourself. If it's bad now and you're in the debt cycle, look at why before making promises to sort it out. If you can get to the root cause, you'll find the path out much easier. If it's good, then ensure it stays that way, and take the necessary steps to maintain that healthy relationship.

> Now let's look at the FEAR.
> This generally comes from edging out
> of your comfort zone –
> I felt it when I started out so I'm
> damn sure the majority of you
> reading this book have too!

I was terrified when I first made the leap into the self-employed/business owner world, after being an employee for so long. All I kept saying to myself was, "What if it all goes wrong and I can't pay the bills?" My daughter was still at school, and as a single mum with no input from elsewhere, I was the breadwinner, I was the sole provider, so, what if it all went tits up, what then?! I look back now and realise that actually my fear came from my poor relationship with money when I was growing up.

Don't get me wrong, I'm not going to give you a sad story about having no cash and a downtrodden home life; I was very lucky to have come from a family who were "comfortable", and I had an amazing childhood.

So what was my issue?

My father worked abroad, so every month he would send money home. It was in the currency of where he was working, not pounds and pence, so some months we would gain and some months we would lose. Then when he came home on leave, he would bring "leave pay" – this was bonus time, this would mean new cars, flash meals, new clothes and so on. You see the pattern here: our money ebbed and flowed, and that's how I had started to live my adult life too.

If I got a bonus from work, that would be a holiday or something new. I was also a borrower, not the short type that live under the floorboards, but a credit card problem-borrower and this had led to a pretty poor credit rating and a personal bankruptcy, because when money got short, that's how I handled it. I had to deal with that bad relationship before starting my business, otherwise I'd be up shit creek and back in employment again before I knew it!

I had to face my fear of running out of money and smelling of dog shit. I had to get my head in order, and plan, making sure I had my personal cash and business cash separate, and knowing about each penny and each pound, where it was going and when. I couldn't afford to let my poor relationship with money kill my business.

There's no shaming here, it's simply about sorting out your head first. If you're already in the journey, check in with yourself and ensure you have this part right, so any future mishaps with money are avoided.

OK, now we have that clear, what about The DREAM?

This beauty is where we all start, and this is usually what the experts call our "WHY". It's something I wholeheartedly encourage you to stay in touch with all the way on your journey, something you never lose sight of, and the one thing you revisit every day, week, month, and year. Sadly, it can be the making or breaking of you and your business beyond the money, hence stay in touch with it and make sure the reality keeps it alive.

So, what exactly is the DREAM? It's the idea - as I said, it's your reason why - the great idea you had for starting your business, your "lightbulb" moment, the moment you decided to start your business, what it would be, whether providing a service or manufacturing a product. It's the conception of how it would work, where it would start, and the result and impact it would have on the world and ultimately your life.

After all, it's about YOU and your "WHY" - it's your dream and yours alone. You know how it's all going to come together and how it can work, it's brilliant, it's going to give you the life you have dreamed of for so long, you may even become a millionaire one day, or just be happy in your world.

> All you need to do is spring into action and get the wheels in motion and, hey presto! You'll be "Living the Dream"!

Ha, so here's the thing, not that I'm a Negative Nelly, but do you know how many times I see this dream go tits up? (Yeah, I know, I love that phrase... but it says it how it is.)

Way too many.

Too many business owners fail before they've even started and it's heart-breaking. No one sets out to fail, but to make the dream a reality, you have to tick all the boxes and not turn your dream into a fairy tale. It's too easy to get carried away and think it's all going to be plain sailing... but even the best entrepreneurs and business owners have fallen flat on their faces at some point.

You're going to hear me say this a lot during this book, but the key to keeping the dream alive is in the PLANNING: the structure to the plan, the careful implementation and not straying from the plan, and ensuring that plan encompasses all areas of the business – not just the sexy Sales and Marketing – the WHOLE of it.

The one big fat fail I see time and time again, the dream-killer, the one area that stamps all over your dream in its big fat boots is... you guessed it: "THE NUMBERS"!

> If I was given a penny for every time I've heard "My Accountant does that for me," I swear I would be a millionaire a million times over.
> To be perfectly honest, I'm bored with hearing it, and it shows a total lack of business awareness.
> There, I've said it:
> I've been wanting to say that brutally honest statement for years!

The Financials of your business are just as important - no, in fact MORE important than the Sales and Marketing, and if you don't take ownership of them now, then your dream can easily turn into a distant memory or even a nightmare. If you really want to make your dream come true, then make sure you understand how to manage and track cash, and how to read and question your Profit & Loss and Balance Sheet.

They are not some mysterious things that appear once a year and only an Accountant can create or understand. They are the KEY to unlocking your dream. Get this right now, and you'll be winning.

Recap:

1. Do you have a healthy relationship with money, or do you need to work on it?

2. What do you need to do right now to ensure that your relationship with money is respectful?

3. Do you live in fear of not having money or do you think you are a natural provider?

4. How do you manage your money now? Are you a bank account checker or a cash manager?

5. Is your Dream your WHY?

6. Are you very clear on your Dream and how it will work?

7. Do you understand how the Financials of your business can help your business Grow?

Chapter 3

Planning: Create your Life P&L

I can hear you now: "What on Earth is she talking about now?"

Your "Life Profit & Loss", that's what I'm talking about. It's not all about business, it's about what you want too. If you don't have a Life Profit & Loss, then why are you in business?

I understand you are in business to make money, but what do you want that money to do for you? It's not purely just to be handed over to HMRC or the IRS, I'm guessing you want some of it too. So what's your plan and how will it ultimately enhance your life?

We all start with "the great idea" for a business. We have this wonderful vision of how we are going to make millions, or improve our lives or even someone else's. It's very rare that there is no end goal, but how do you ensure you keep hold of that dream and hit that goal. What will be the drivers to ensure you hit the goal, how will you measure it, what will success look like and so on. All these are important factors of your Life P&L.

> The saddest thing I have seen over the years is the number of business owners that have never even had a Life P&L, let alone a Business Plan, so they end up on the scrap heap of tired business owners,

or the business falls flat on its face within the five-year marker. They started their dream business with absolutely no clue what life was going to hold for them, or if they could actually make the business work, so it was very much on a wing and a prayer.

A Business Plan doesn't have to be all woo-woo and vision boards, you can create your plan in a one-page Word document or a spreadsheet, or you can draw it in your favourite pad in felt tip pen, or even on the back of a fag packet if you must (although I don't recommend this one – something a little larger if I were you!) but please don't skip this important part of Business Planning.

So whilst you are thinking about your business and creating this great dream of changing the world or the planet, let's just reel it in a bit. Let's look at you and what you want as your end goal and where it all fits in.

When I started my business, I was determined never to

become an employee ever again. I was fed up with the corporate world, its hang ups, the pressure to deliver unreasonable and unachievable budgets, and never seeing my family. I was that crappy single parent that could never make sports days or parents' evenings as I had a deadline to meet, or I was out of the country on business, so for me, it was about me and my life and giving back to my life.

> I don't believe in the concept of "work/life balance", it's bullshit to be honest.

You'll work harder in your own business then you ever will as an employee, but you can create a better life for yourself if you're like me and that's what you want.

I also wanted financial freedom. Even having the lovely fat corporate salary, it never seemed enough, and payday could never come around fast enough. So I wanted to break that bad habit and have the money to have a good life without counting every penny, or being desperate at the end of the month. I was done with scrimping for holidays but never quite having the holiday I wanted, and having to turn down nights out with friends because it was too close to the end of the month.

I was very clear on what I wanted: I wanted a life where I actually enjoyed working – yes, I may have to work hard but ultimately, I could be flexible with my working time if my family needed me, or I simply wanted to spend time with them, then I could allow myself that flexibility.

So the first part of my Life P&L was about having time and capacity for my work to fit in around ME. I mapped out the amount of hours I wanted to work; I don't mind working weekends as I don't believe business is all 9am-5pm, it just doesn't work. Your clients most likely won't be nine-to-five, especially if they live outside your time zone, so I knew I needed to be flexible to make life work for me. It meant that I could do the odd Spa day, or have lunch with my daughter if I wanted to, without feeling guilty and telling myself I should be at my desk, or checking emails constantly and trying to juggle my own time.

The second part for me was around having financial freedom, so again, I mapped this out. I made sure that I, as the Most Important Employee of my Business (we look at this in Chapter 7), was going to be paid what I wanted in order to create that freedom. I mapped out the holidays I wanted, the house I wanted, the car – the whole shebang – so I knew exactly what I wanted and I was very clear on this.

This isn't about leasing a car through the business, or a putting a holiday through the books as a "business trip". All this does is overload your business before you even start, and the thing is, you still have to earn that money. I have seen this happen: the greedy business owner who believes they are there to just "run" the business, and bleeds it dry with the excessive lifestyle that the business can't afford. This scenario was never going to be me.

I urge you to seriously think about this if you think being an entrepreneur or self-employed business owner is just about a swanky lifestyle, flash car, big house and private schools. It can be, but – and I mean BUT – you have to earn it. Beware the "dividend scenario" or taking from your business. You'll end up paying a huge amount of tax for borrowing from your business, and it's frowned upon by our tax friends and the banks alike. Behave like this, and not only are you a bad risk, but a fool to yourself too.

Anyway, I digress. Yes, map all these lovely things out. It's about achieving your goals, having the plan and creating the dream journey with your business being the driver of all the things you want without being a burden to your business. No doubt you will be different to me and have different goals so just get clear on what you want and do the same: map it out.

I did actually create a vision board as I'm a visual person so wanted to see these things in colour and big and bold. OK, I admit it's a bit woo-woo and the whole "manifestation trip" but believe me, it worked.

Well, not all of it. I did have a picture of James Martin the Yorkshire Chef on my board, but he is yet to fall at my feet! However, I do now have the car I wanted, and the house, and yes, I have holidays when I want. So this shit works – but I worked for it all, and I planned it too.

Oh, and don't be fooled: it doesn't stop when you've achieved some of these things — or all of them —you keep this going for as long as you are in business, as you are the driver within your business.

You may even have family working for you: I do, and yep, it was in my plan! It was always one of my dreams to be able to provide a job for my daughter, and something that a few years ago would have been merely a pipe dream, but sure enough, eighteen months into owning and running my own business, I needed some support with marketing and, lo and behold, my daughter had just finished her Degree and I could offer her a role within what is now our "family business".

At the time of writing this book, we are planning her own part of the business too, so we are getting clear on my daughter's plan and goals (yes, Proud Mum moment!) and of course she's following our:
Business Planning 101 course
https://sallybrady.co.uk/business-planning-101/

If your business is a Community Interest Company or a Charity, you will have a vision for this too, so the process and theory are no different: what does the vision look like? Map it out. If you are a charity or a

CIC even, the vision may be to make a small or a large impact in your chosen area, or maybe it's to change the world – why not? If that's your aim, do it! Imagine how you will feel when you achieve that goal. Write down and describe how you think it will feel too, as it really helps you visualise, and then when you are near, or have hit that goal – I'm pretty sure I'll be applauding you! Don't stop there, set another goal. Keep going and you'll keep driving your business forward, making a bigger and bigger impact.

People really do forget this part, or don't even think about it. If you have been asked to create a Business Plan for a start-up loan, or any business loan by a grant funding board or bank, this part is never even mentioned.

You may be asked about salary, but this is more than just salary; this is ultimately WHY you are in business. You'll be asked to create an Executive Summary, a Sales and Marketing Plan and a Cashflow, but I can guarantee they won't ask you what you want or how your life may be changed by your business, yet it's the fundamental reason you are in business. So for me, it's one of the major, if not THE major part of Business Planning.

This isn't something that's just for start-ups or sole traders either. This is for all business owners, so even if you are currently in business and may have been for a few years, sit down and look at your Life P&L for the next few years. You may look at selling the business or retiring, or you may be looking to increase turnover and profitability massively. So how will you achieve it?

What will all this mean to you and your life?

If you have family in the business, ask them to do the same and see if your visions align. You may be surprised and find your kids or siblings have a vision for the future you never even imagined! It's so important to factor YOU into your business and your outcomes.

Losing sight of that dream is often a very sad road. Not everyone fails because they don't have a dream but you will hear the sad tales of having been in business for years and wondering why. Don't get me wrong, there are also those who fall completely on their feet, never plan a thing, and make millions. But they are rare, and whilst I champion their success, I would ask, "What's next? You've made your millions, how are you going to maintain it? What's the plan?"

I created a YouTube video on this a while ago now. It's only ten minutes long but it's a summary of all of the above and what to think about when starting your business journey or if you're already on your business journey.

The link is here: https://youtu.be/_SQ6O97yHPM. I also cover this with all my clients, whether you work with me 1:1 or you join my **Business Planning 101** course https://sallybrady.co.uk/business-planning-101/.

You'll cover this section, and as I keep wittering on, it's so important to get this part well and truly factored into your Business Plan and review it regularly, don't forget it and don't think that once you've achieved one goal, it will stop there. Even if you have made millions, as I said earlier, you still have to maintain it. It could only take another worldwide disaster like the Covid pandemic, and you could lose the lot, so be prepared, have your "what next" and your goals firmly cemented into your plan and review them daily, weekly, monthly, and yearly.

> *P.S. I'm still hoping James Martin will jump off my page!*

Recap:

1. Create your own Life P&L, using what works for you: use vision boards or write it down, but be really clear on what you want from your business.

2. How you will integrate your Life P&L into your business.

3. Have a "what next" plan, always be thinking about your next step.

4. When do you want to retire? It's an important feature of your plan.

Sally Brady

Chapter 4

Preparing Your Plan

In Chapter 1, I talked about the Business Plan being built of lots of different elements and that each chapter of this book will cover everything you need to build your Business Plan. So far, I have covered:

1. What is a Business Plan and why do you need one?

2. Why many small businesses fail within the first five years.

3. Your Life P&L.

These are all chapters preparing you for building your Business Plan, getting your head in the space ready to build a solid plan and not a fag packet wafty one.

On my **Business Planning 101** course, I always start in the same way: I prepare you for building the plan. We look at relationships around money first as this is a key part for any business owner. As I have already said, a poor relationship with personal money will feed negatively into your business too.

The prior preparation is key as we all know, "Piss-poor preparation leads to piss-poor planning," or as I state in Module 2 of my course, the seven P's of planning: "Proper Planning and Preparation Prevents Piss-Poor Performance". The first chapters of this book are doing exactly that, getting you ready to plan effectively.

So many business owners believe that it's all about the sexy Sales and Marketing, and I spent the whole of my Accounting career being told by arrogant salespeople that they paid my salary. Nice I know, and if you are a business owner who is a salesperson, this is where I get to show you some home truths,

> as whilst sales are the element that drive turnover, they do not – and let me repeat that for you again – they do NOT drive profit

... wow, that felt good (sorry spikey moment, I've wanted to do that for years!!!)

On a serious note, sales do not drive profit if you don't know your costs, overheads included. You can make all the sales in the world, but if you do not have a handle on your costs, then they are just a vanity metric in your business.

I know sales are lovely, and so is marketing if that is in your DNA, and yes of course, if you can sell sand to the Arabs then you are a winner! But please for the love of me, make sure you know the costs of your business, so when you start your plan in the next chapter, think of me as a parrot on your shoulder and hear my dulcet northern tones reminding you to know your costs too.

I am certainly not asking you to be unambitious in your Sales and Marketing plan, and I'm not asking you to hold back your sales demon. I am just asking you to be aware of your costs, it's

NOT KNOWING these costs that can be the killer of profit.

I hear it time and time again: turnover is great but in the same breath, the phrase "my sales are up and my turnover is on par, but I don't have any money and I'm not even making a profit..." That's simply because you don't know your costs, that's all, but you won't believe how many times I hear that statement.

Even the larger businesses I've worked with over the

last few years can always tell me their turnover within a nano-second, but when I ask if they know their direct costs, or cost of sales, I usually hit an uncomfortable and business-owner-embarrassing silence. So if you are a start-up reading this book, get a grip of this now and don't have that embarrassing silence with me, and if you are an established business owner, get a grip of this now before I ask you that question.

The same goes for when you are looking at your marketing strategy and building this part of your Business Plan, make sure that your marketing strategy and your sales plan align to the growth and profitability of your business.

Marketing is a huge factor in the growth of your business as it's getting your face and brand awareness out there, and here comes the "but" again: if you are spending zillions on marketing blindly, you will blow any sign of profit out of the water, so make sure you have a keen eye on your marketing strategy.

Being caught by the latest shiny marketing tool or the coach who costs you £$5K per session but has no proven strategy or can't give you social proof or does not meet your budget, is a pointless exercise. You will be on a hiding to losses.

Yes of course, we all make marketing mistakes, but we learn and learn quickly. Think before committing your whole budget to one person or one campaign, spread the love and create a marketing strategy that works for your product or service and serves your brand.

I personally believe in having a clear marketing strategy and have no issue with investing in my business for the purpose of driving sales, but I always align the plan to the possible outcomes; if you can't afford the shiny coach who costs you £$5K right now – don't! Look at a solution to help you build up to that position, look at possibly creating it yourself or look locally for more affordable options, so again, when you are planning your marketing, think about the costs involved and the impacts this may have. I go into this in more detail in the next chapter where you start building your plan.

> Now I'm going to give you an insight into the really sexy part of the business and the real driver.

As I've already stated, the majority of you believe it's the "sexy Sales and Marketing". Wrong, just WRONG! The really sexy bit is CASH! Yep you heard it right here and right now, CASH is the sexy beast in business, it is the one thing that no business can survive without, and when you can handle this beast, you are well and truly winning. If you can tame this beast and make it work for you, it will blow your mind. They don't call me "Sally Brady the #Cashflowlady" for no reason.

All joking aside, it is the one part of your business that, when you can control cash and make it work for you, you will always be in a good position. I go into minute detail in Chapters 9 and 10 of this book about building and maintaining Cashflow.

This is so simple and effective to all businesses, big or small, but again, one of the fundamentals that gets missed by so many. Creating the cash in the first place is the more difficult part as, to have cash, you have to generate a profit. The key is, once you have that cash, control it, eke it out, make it work for you, not the other way around. Having a simple Cashflow Forecast that you maintain every week will tell you if you are making a profit; if the cash starts to go down, it will be because you are not generating profit, and you can go from there to investigate why.

Whatever you do, do not skip this part of the planning and don't assume you can live without a Cashflow Forecast.

> You'll be paddling around like a duck with one leg and going nowhere if you cannot manage your cash; bank account glancing and guessing will not cut it.

Take it from an expert: it's not difficult to do and I provide my students with simple templates to help them build their forecasts. I do not believe in making it complex as you just won't keep it up, you'll find it cumbersome and annoying, and it will get left behind and you'll eventually be that one-legged duck.

As we have now established, this is the most important part of running a business. Make a mental and physical note now to always have this area of your business on point, so if you meet me in the street one day and I ask if you have a Cashflow Forecast, you'll say, "Yes of course Sally, I'm not your average business owner, I'm a successful business owner. I don't just have a Business Plan, I have a damn good Cashflow Forecast too," and I'll drop all my shopping to give you a big fat hurrah!! Now that's something to really look forward to for you and me!!!

Before you begin the next chapters and start building your Business Plan, just take a moment to think about the first four chapters and what I have already talked about: are you ready for this world of business and what you can achieve? Are you wholeheartedly ready for the ups and downs, the countless hours and stress you are about to embark on? If you are a start-up, you can run for the hills now and if you're already in business, you'll know exactly what I am saying. The world of business is hard, it's tough, it can be thankless, but at the end of the day,

> *if you do this with 100% commitment, it can be the most gratifying and satisfying place you will ever be.*

You will work harder than you ever did as an employee, but the end goal is yours and no one else's, you work for YOU.

There will be times where you are banging your head on a desk wondering why you started; you will want to throw in the towel every week; you'll talk about getting out and getting a job; your family will whinge at you for not being there and working so much; you'll get asked why you don't just get a job; why as a business owner you can't just drop everything during the day and go for lunch or head out early to meet a mate. No one will ever get it like you do. It's a lonely place at times, if you are planning to employ staff they will never have the love and commitment for your business that you do, so drop that expectation right now, it's yours and yours alone.

> I stated in Chapter 3 that you are the driver within your business, and this will always be the case until you retire or exit.

You will always be at the head of the table; don't be a hobbyist, be a proud business owner and make this the most successful thing (besides kids - well mine was an achievement in that she survived my shit parenting and turned out pretty damn great!) you've ever done in your life. You may only get one crack at this game, if you fail you may stand to lose a lot, so all I'm saying here is give this your all.

If you are a start-up, you have started from a good place. By reading this book, you are clearly wanting to build a plan and ensure you get off on the right foot. If you are already established, I'm pretty sure you are looking at why and how a plan can help you. Even if you are currently profitable, you'll have that "what next?" and "how do I stay profitable?" question running around in your head, so now is the time to discover the next step.

> Here endeth my questioning and lecture. My main point here is to be straight with yourself and don't cheat at any point, as you'll only cheat yourself.

The next eight chapters will take you through step-by-step how to build that all-important plan, with a little of my crappy wit and humour along the way. Everything I talk about and show you is something I have done and currently do in my own business.

My beliefs are integrity and visibility in all that I do so that when I'm teaching, I can demonstrate from a place of knowledge, not theory. So as those crappy coaches always tell you: "Trust the process." (That one's almost as bad as "Pivot"!) Anyway, crack on. Give your all and let me know how you get on...

Recap:

1. It's not all about Sales and Marketing.

2. CASH is the true sexy beast in business.

3. To have CASH you need to make a profit. Ensure you know your costs.

4. Sally will give you a massive hug if you always track your cash.

5. Be clear in what you want before you start your business.

6. GET PLANNING.

Chapter 5

Marketing

So, the bit I know you all love, the part everyone thinks is the lifeblood of the Business Plan. Of course, you know I'll disagree because the lifeblood is the Financials!

> However to make the blood flow, we need some sales, and to create sales we need marketing.

I'm sure you've all come into contact at some stage with a fabulous marketeer, or you know of a big marketing agency and see the wonderful brand creation and advertising campaigns they bring to life in magazines, on television, on billboards and so on. This does NOT have to be you. You don't need a massive marketing budget to start your campaign and you don't need to have a huge bowl of marketing knowledge to start with.

I certainly didn't, and it hasn't stopped my business growing and evolving. I did choose branding colours and a logo that sat with me, and at that time it didn't cost the earth but I did stay "on brand" as they say, so that I was recognisable as I started to show up.

At the start, the biggest part of your marketing budget is you and your time, the rest can be free! Social Media is free, organic growth is free – the part that costs is the paid advertising, and if you choose this route, my advice here would be to speak to an expert first, as it can be a very costly mistake. Yes, I have tried that one and luckily I had an expert in my corner who swooped in and stopped me in my tracks before it cost me the earth. Since then I chose to grow organically, it's a choice.

Social Media is a tricky little animal too when it comes to family and friends.

> I have lost count of the times I've rolled my eyes at the comments and the "When are you getting a proper job?" Jibes, along with "What are you doing, I keep seeing your posts?"

Friends and family can be your biggest champions and your worst critics, so I keep my Social Media platforms for personal and business separate now. I didn't to start with, but I fast learnt the family lesson and decided I didn't want the comments, or to saturate my friends and family with my content and sales posts.

In this chapter, I talk mainly about Social Media as this is where I have had most of my success in generating sales, but you may want to use external input or other forms of brand advertising.

Either way, if you are looking to grow, Social Media platforms are a no-brainer. Over the years I have had varying forms of advice in terms of which platforms to use; some say use them all, some say pick a couple and forget the rest.

Personally, I have found LinkedIn and Instagram are my arenas. I'm not a fan of Facebook or Twitter since at the time of writing this book, they are both platforms with their own issues and I just haven't felt that vibe.

For information videos, I use YouTube, so feel free to check out my YouTube channel and subscribe. I use TikTok for short fun and informative videos, so pick what works for you, and of course,

> do feel free to connect with me on any of the platforms as I would love to hear your story and follow your journey too!

Once you know which platforms are for you, then do your audience research: who is going to buy your product and service and why, really get to know who they are. Most marketeers will get you to draw Jonny or Jenny and their five kids, big house in the country, their BMW 5 series, what they eat, where they eat and what entertainment they like, and so on.

> To be honest I've found this part useless and did not help me in my business at all, as Jonny and Jenny may be into whips and chains and a bit of S&M and I'm trying to sell them Business services... hmm OK, there may be a Business Plan in there, but not sure we are on the same page!

What I did find useful was knowing who I wanted to work with and why, so I built my pillars. I'm very much about honesty and integrity and visibility, so I wanted to work with business owners who fit in with my own morals and beliefs. They may not be living the same dream, but they want to, or they may not be doing it now but the desire is there. They may be struggling with Cashflow, may be massively in debt, but they need a way out and I can provide that.

I give them support and show them how easy it is to build a Cashflow and manage it and see the light at the end of the tunnel. Maybe they are starting up, or already have a great business or business idea, but need a plan for the future, or even need funding.
Yep I have a solution for that... you see what I'm doing here? I'm building my client profile, my niche, and what they need from me.

Really think about your "Why". To quote Simon Sinek, an inspirational author and speaker: "Why are you doing what you do and why would someone buy from you?" Lots of whys, but if you keep telling yourself why, you'll soon sit more comfortably with what your business is, why you started and who you want to sell to, and then the Marketing and Selling starts to roll much more easily. If you don't know your why or your niche, you won't sell effectively as you won't speak about your business with confidence or clarity.

Once you've honed down the whys and the kind of client you want to work with, as I said, you'll speak with confidence and clarity and be able to start building your audience. To do that, you need to be out there making yourself known and voicing your expertise loudly and proudly, and most of all, consistently.

I was once told by a member of my local Chamber of Commerce that I was a bit of a legend in the area and very well known. I had no idea of my building reputation; all I can say is that I am out there consistently showing up to my audience – very much like the performing seal!

So, how did I do it?

I started to write content consistently and post it on my chosen platforms, talking about me and my business, showcasing my services and prodding the pain of my potential clients. Of course, it's scary at first and you'll hit the "post" button and run for the hills, but it gets easier and easier, and you gain in confidence the more you write. This is why I say

"Know your business and know your audience"

as you are the expert, and you are showing them the way to buying from you. You don't need to be all salesy on every post and you certainly don't need to post ten times a day on ten different platforms, but what you do need is to show your expertise and to be consistent.

I won't lie, it took me over a year to start getting consistent leads through LinkedIn, and even now, I can tell if I'm dropping the ball. I measure my stats and know I've been a lazy arse and pull my big-girl pants on and get on with it! Consistency is showing up at least three times a week with good solid content, showing your personality and your business as a leader.

Don't post about Bessie starting school this week, or your dog having its first shit. I'll be brutally honest here: no one cares. What they want to know is who you are and why they should buy from you.

> Needling the pain point of your prospective customer is the best bit of advice I ever received.

Then you show how you can solve their pain. Really make their eyes water in the first part of your post and then show them a nice simple solution. You don't need to sell here, just show your expertise.

You're not giving away all your secrets, you're just showing them how simple you can make life for them and that you're the expert they need in their life, and you're walking them through something that hurts – but you've got them.

Find some great content writers on your chosen platforms; follow them, learn from then, look at their style and adapt it for yourself and your strategy.

> Do not – and I cannot stress this enough – DO NOT plagiarise! You'll get caught out and it's not good.

Just learn and adapt and you'll find your own way easily enough. Don't overthink any of this or keep editing and re-editing and comparing; these guys started where you are now and hey, we all make mistakes, so just learn, learn and learn again.

Next part is the face-to-face. Find a networking group that you like and build the relationships. Again, don't go in there all salesy and expecting Fred the Aerial Man to buy from you as soon as you shake his hand. Build the relationship, get to know him and build the trust. I'm sure you've heard the saying "know, like and trust".

Again, this is a no-brainer. The other one is "It's not who you know, it's who they know". This is a magical one as when people start to know, like and trust you, and have confidence that you'll do a good job, they might not use you but I'm damn sure they'll recommend you, and therein start the referrals.

Personally, I'm not a fan of the networking groups that force referrals or have "closed" groups.

> If you impose rules on me I'll behave like a petulant child and spend my time on the naughty step. I like the relaxed, getting-to-know-you style of networking.

My local Chamber of Commerce do monthly visits to interesting businesses like vineyards, or climbing experiences, and I love this as I learn about the business, and you then have a commonality to chat with the other business owners, and before you know it, you're easing into make great connections and doing business.

I was also a leader of a smaller networking group that supported smaller businesses. I love the support and relationships there, some have become friends too. I do chuckle sometimes at the immediate "Buy from me" sixty-second pitch in both smaller and more established businesses so please don't do it, just tell a story about something that's relevant to your business. People like a story they can relate to and you'll gain trust.

> *If there is one lesson I can give you in all of this, it's "Consistency".*

If you do go networking, put it in your diary every week, build it into your marketing strategy and show up every week. Don't make excuses and don't put client visits or meetings over networking. You need to be consistently growing and maintaining your business to keep a consistent flow of clients and business.

I see all too often the businesses who have the feast-

and-famine approach to marketing, and only do it when the business or money starts to dry up, and that's when the desperation I talked about earlier in this book kicks in, and that, as we know, "smells like dog shit". This is your business and you need to show up.

> Finally, last but certainly by no means least, know your competition!

You may think you're unique, and I hate to burst your bubble – but you're not. There will be someone out there, big or small, doing what you do, so you just need to know who they are and do it better. I don't mean compare yourself and get all hung up, I mean find a little something that they might not do, or find a corner of the market they have missed, or even just Be You.

No one else is you after all, and no one will do what you do in your style, so don't feel compelled to mimic your competition, just be good at what you do, and for heaven's sake, don't ever slag off the competition, you'll make yourself look bitter and twisted.
Just walk tall and Be You and don't be drawn into pointless competition battles as no one wins these.

OK, so where does this all fit in the Business Plan? Everything I have talked about in this chapter is about building and creating your Sales and Marketing strategy and how to do it, so this is exactly what you build into your Business Plan: the How, What, Where and When outlined in detail in your plan. Talk about all this in fine detail so that you are very much focused on what you are selling and to whom.

Build into your Social Media plan and strategy, how often you are going to post and where, which networking groups you are going to attend and why, who your customer is and why, and so on. Get clear and be specific, even build in your client avatar (Jonny and Jenny if that's your thing!)

Remember, whether this plan is for you to focus on the future of your business, or you are looking for funding or grants, you need to be clear and succinct. We don't do wishy-washy planning here, it's all in the detail and strategy.

> Another tip: every touch-point you have in life is a potential sale for your business, so think beyond the tips I have given in this chapter, even get all blue-sky if you want.

I won't beat you up for this out-of-the-box way, I'll champion what works for you, so again, share your journey with me, I love to learn new ways of thinking, even if it is blue-sky. ;)

Recap:

1. What is your business and what are you selling?

2. Who is your client and why?

3. Why should they buy from you?

4. What are your chosen Social Media platforms and why?

5. What is your marketing strategy plan detail?

6. Who is your competition and why?

Chapter 6

Sales

OK, so now we are clear on what your business is and what you are selling, who your client is, why they should buy from you, who your competition is, Social Media platforms you are going to use and why, and there you are: you've created a marketing strategy and plan in detail. We now need to look at the sales in more detail.

Most people start with a base product, or one service, and put all their efforts and focus into that one area. That is where you can easily go wrong.

Having only one item or one service to sell can be difficult, and it can also lead to a very unpleasant place of dependency. Having one product generally means one type of customer to sell to, and only one income stream.

Don't get me wrong, it's a good place to start; as with everything in this world, we all have to start somewhere and after all, we need an income and sales to start the ball of profit rolling.

> My point is, one base product or service can lead to having all your eggs in one basket, and yep, guess what? I've seen this a lot too.

When the market suddenly decides your income stream is not a good one, or not on-trend, or it's a luxury, you're stuffed. Sales decline, and costs can increase, so profit is out of the window. The other side to this is your one base product can lead to one big customer, and you get all comfy, your profit margin with them is good, the relationship is all hunky-dory and life is good...

No, no, NO! They suddenly get tempted away by a competitor, you start to haggle, the profit margins are squeezed, your competitor has a better edge than you and can buy materials cheaper, or they are a slightly better service provider than you. You made a couple of mistakes they didn't forget, they may have forgiven but, lo and behold, suddenly they are talking about it again and boom! They've moved supplier or service provider and you are left out in the cold... remember this:

> "Loyalty costs"

You got so comfortable with this one big customer you neglected your marketing strategy, you didn't feel the need to post regularly on Social Media, you had it nailed, you didn't have time to market, they were eating your time, your smaller customers were OK, they didn't need your attention, and to be honest it didn't matter that they went elsewhere, they didn't deliver the margin like this one, plus you've got others, and hey ho, life will be fine... but it's not, is it? You have wages to pay, suppliers who need their money too.

You bought the materials in advance not anticipating this situation, or you booked out your time and didn't think the other customers would mind waiting, and here you are – left with one almighty great hole in your business.

> The worst case of this I have seen was a business owner literally being wiped out overnight with debts to pay and no form of income.

They had believed this would never happen, they had got way too dependent and had not marketed at all, and now had nothing. There was no explanation, no sweet goodbye, just a "We don't need your services anymore" scenario. No notice was given as no contract was in place, so it was a very bitter end to a long and fruitful relationship and – oh look: there's the bankruptcy boat calling.

Do not blame everyone else in this scenario, you have only one person to blame here, and that's you. Never get so comfortable that you think the sun will shine on you every day. It won't. It rains and sometimes it pours, and it's shit if you haven't worked with more than one customer and more than one income stream.

Spread the love: you can have the big customer, just don't have ONE, and don't make the excuse of not having time to service other customers. If you are going to have this customer, you need to ensure you plan more hours into your day and work at weekends to make it fit with your other customers.

Now, let's talk income streams.

Basically, you need more than one. One is not enough. It won't help you grow, you'll stifle yourself and you'll stagnate. You'll see in many business coaching books and online advice to have at least three income streams, and I wholeheartedly agree with this approach.

It leads to a more balanced and consistent income stream within your business. Not all will be as profitable but they all will contribute to your end goal.

> If you are manufacturing or reselling a product, think about products to complement the main product you have.

For example, if you are manufacturing, could there be a by-product made from waste, or if it's a relatively expensive product, could you offer something at a slightly lower cost that complements it in some way and which could service a different customer group than your main core product.

The same goes if you are a reseller of products: think about department stores. They have high, medium and low-end brands to suit all budgets, and this is what you are ultimately aiming for too so that you can capture as much of the market share as possible.

> If you offer a service, what is your core service, and what could you do to ensure that whilst you are hitting your main customer base, you also have a steady income stream coming in?

Sometimes the higher-value clients can come and go, and also take time to convert as you are asking a higher price and therefore the decision can take longer to make. If, in the meantime, you have another income stream building, you can keep your costs covered.

> The lower-costing income stream is the one that is always good to have to cover your overheads,

the main costs of the business, so at any one time you have enough coming in, regardless of the big deals.

These are the cherry on the top of your business, they are ultimately what you set out to do, whereas the lower-cost product or service is a good one but a necessary one to keep you going.

The third income stream is the middle ground. It's slightly better than the lower cost one but not the cream on the pie, or the cherry on top of the main product or service you sell. You'll hear some retailers or service providers talk about "done for you" and "done with you" services as income streams, so a "done for you" is where (as it says on the tin) the customer does nothing and the provider delivers the full service or suite of products, purely bespoke. This is what I am describing as the "cherry on the top" scenario, the crème de la crème of product or service.

The "done with you" scenario will cost slightly less and the customer will do a lot of the work or have a slightly lower standard of product and be guided by the supplier.

We can look at this in the context of supermarkets. I speak from experience having worked for a manufacturer of food and pharmaceutical products in my heyday. The "high-end" supermarket own-brands have a better product content than the lower end, hence if you buy a headache pill from the high-end supermarket it may cost you £1, whereas the lower-end product will cost you 30p. However, the actual product made and distributed by the brand manufacturer will be priced at £1.50.

All will have the same product ingredients but marketed in different packaging and therefore given a different consideration by the consumer. What we are looking at here is three income streams, high, middle and low, all contributing to the profit of the business.

The key now is to apply a similar theory to your business product or service.

What could you do that would give you three income streams, one to cover costs and/or overheads, one to make a slightly higher margin, and one other to give a big fat Yes Please margin? Don't over complicate it, no blue-sky thinking please, just plain old common sense to give you a good strong profitable income.

Sometimes as your business progresses, the lower-end product starts to really take off and its volumes become more profitable than you expected. This can apply to both service and product areas of business, and if it does, great, you're onto an absolute winner.

> I'll give you an example of my own business. As I'm writing this book, we have three income streams.

The first is an inexpensive "done for you" service in which we support businesses with the day-to-day finances of their business and help with cash planning and forecasting.

Then we have the **Business Planning 101** course. This is a "done with you" service as you complete the six modules of the course online, but you have a weekly group call with me directly, to help you build your Business Plan. The call comprises of a Q&A session and also a group learning where I teach you something around planning and business relative to setting out the week ahead.

I have a Consultancy business too which is the third income stream. Here I work with businesses on a 1:1 basis, either weekly or monthly, and that is my higher cost income stream as ultimately, you are working with me and tapping into my expertise on an exclusive basis.

All are valuable services.

This is something I would really like to instil in you: none of the products or services you offer should be below par in your eyes.

All the services or products you supply are valuable, it's just at what level your expertise or knowledge is being utilised, or how much of the base materials you are utilising. If you are like me, you may have decades of experience you are giving access to, which took a lot of time and effort to gain.

That knowledge is valuable and not easily come by and it takes a long time to gain, so to benefit from that expertise on a 1:1 basis will, of course, cost more, but if you choose to join my course, you are sharing the cost of my time with others.

The "done for you" scenario for me has been capped as we can only allocate so much time to this area before we lose the personal touch. One thing I always promised myself was that I would pride myself in ensuring that my clients could talk to me when they needed to, and

Sally Brady

I would support them without compromising myself by allowing the services to get so big that they had to outsourced.

Therefore, I outsource other areas of the business and cap this income stream to a level where it covers the costs and overheads of the business and provides a reasonable profit. The other income streams can then be more profitable and areas for continuous growth.

> The one thing I never, ever do though, is stop marketing any one of those income streams.

You need a pipeline of prospective clients at all times to be able to fill any gaps as they arise. You never know when a business may change direction, or decide they don't want to work with you any more.

I never, ever assume a client will be with me forever as that is just pure vanity, and business does not work like that. Business is business, not personal, so you treat it as such.

I stick to my marketing plan at all times and let it evolve to ensure that I am constantly marketing all three income streams. I post on my chosen Social Media platforms; I network online and face to face; I openly talk about my business wherever I go, as every day is a sales opportunity, but I'm not a pushy salesperson – that's not my style. I believe you nurture relationships and I want business to be fun too.

As I said earlier, don't make this a complicated overthought process. You may start with a couple of income streams which will evolve or even change as you change and grow, just don't place all your faith in one income stream and one customer – that's business suicide.

Recap:

1. Define your base product or service.

2. Create at least two more income streams.

3. Ensure at least one of these income streams covers your main costs and/or overheads.

4. Do not rely on one "big" customer – spread the love.

5. Cherish all customers, no matter what income stream or category they come into.

6. Market your business at all times, even when you are at capacity, never drop the ball on marketing.

Sally Brady

Chapter 7

The Financials
Part One:
The Personal Cashflow

"You are the most important employee and person in your business within your business". I'll repeat that as it's something you need to get your head around:

> "You are The Most Important
> Employee and
> Person within your business".

Why do I feel the need to say it and repeat it? Because so many business owners I have met over the last few years have told me, "I can't afford to pay myself," or "I'm not paying myself right now as I'm reinvesting in the business".

So let's look at those two statements individually, so

you understand this right now and either avoid making the same mistakes or deal with the situation ASAP.

"I can't afford to pay myself."

What does that statement shout immediately? No doubt you can guess my answer: "Why are you in business then?"

When you set out in business, it's not for the hell of it, it's predominantly to make money. I'm not saying you have to make millions, this is a choice you make. You may just want a lifestyle business where you are comfortable and happy with ticking along and having the comfortable life you dreamed of.

Or you may have formed a CIC or a Charity in which you are just paying yourself for your time and expenses and donating the rest to your cause.

> *Or you may want to be a millionaire.*

This is all about choices, but not one person I know has ever set out in business to have no form of income whatsoever, so when I hear that statement, I generally know there's an issue that needs addressing immediately and it's usually debt or poor cash management, both of which I can show you simple ways to manage.

"I'm not paying myself right now as I'm reinvesting in the business."

> My response to this one is usually, "What a load of bollocks!"

This one simply says to me, "I've made some poor, if not stupid decisions, I've not managed the business Cashflow, I have no plans in place, I'm winging it and I can't be honest with myself. So I'll make a statement that makes me feel good and people will appreciate and think I'm wise!"

The reality is, get a grip and be honest and start looking at what you are doing and start managing the business, and then you WILL be able to pay yourself.

> Don't beat yourself up for the mistakes, learn from them, take action and don't repeat them.

If you are just starting out then the above is something you need to remember and instil in your business and your mindset from Day One. If you're already in business and these excuses are you, then take heed, and feel free to contact me as I can help.

A lot of people ask me why I always get them to do a Personal Cashflow first when doing the Financials as it's "nothing to do with the business", but not having done this is usually why they end up in one or both of the scenarios above.

If you approach a bank or get a bog-standard Business Planning Template online, I know that a Personal Cashflow is never included, but that's where I'm different.

I'm a business owner who started from scratch, and I'm also a financial geek, who's been a single mum with £10 or less to my name and had to manage money down to the last penny, so trust me, I know how important this one is. It is most certainly a huge part of the business as it's about the Most Important Employee – you ARE the business.

When I started my business, I made sure that I knew how much I needed to survive, but also how much I wanted to earn too; I wanted to be comfortable. I was fed up with living beyond my means and waiting for the next pay cheque.

To do that, I needed to understand these needs, as the only way I was going to earn my money was through my business, and that business had to have me at the forefront of its Cashflow, otherwise what was the point of it all?

> I still laugh now when people say to me "Oh just put that expense through your business." Do you know why? Because that business is ME and I still have to earn the money for that expense!

So when you hear things like that, just do what I do and laugh or roll your eyes, as they are the ones who are probably struggling in business, and like me, you'll know why.

For years I had listed and tracked my income and expenses, but like so many of you reading this book now (I think I'm correct in my assumption) I wasn't always one hundred per cent accurate.

Basically I was cheating myself by missing out the odd small Direct Debit or the minor cash expenditure because it didn't really matter, did it, and it made me feel better about my poor cash position.

Yes, yes it did matter and that's why I was always too close to the mark heading to payday!

> So, take a tip from the expert now:
> don't cheat yourself!

These days, I look at it like going to the gym and only doing half a workout; the only person you're cheating is you, so don't do it.

Now I track every penny in and out and I know exactly what I need and when. And yes, I do still manage my Personal Cashflow daily. If you can get into this habit now, you're on a winner.

OK, So Where Do You Start?

It's much simpler than you think so we'll go through the process so that you can get started – oh and feel free to email me and ask questions, as I've said, I'm happy to help you on your journey.

Tools

First step is to choose your tool, or pick your poison as my daughter likes to say. Don't over-complicate this step; if you like pen and paper, use pen and paper. If you like a spreadsheet, use a spreadsheet.

This one is my preference as it's easy to change and update and you don't have to keep scrapping your paper and can keep it all in one place and keep your history much easier.

I'm not a fan of cash forecasting software as I have yet to discover one that I can't find a fault with:

> they can't read your mind or predict your life, so if you're a software developer reading this book, then this could be your challenge!

Whatever you choose, this is for you and no one else. Just make sure it's simple and it's something you will use over and over again, as a

> Cashflow is like a dog – it's not just for Christmas, it's for life!

Gather your Statements

This next part is the painful part, but it's worth every part of the pain as it will ultimately give you your end goal. When you've done it once, it will be much easier to keep track of in the future and I doubt you'll have to do it again, although I do recommend reviewing at least once a year.

Go and find all your bank statements and credit card statements for the past year. If you have to contact your bank and pay a fee for the old statements, it's worth it. You may find things you only spend on once a year and without the history you may miss it.

Once you have all the information gathered, you are ready for the really, really painful bit. (I actually find this the best bit! I'm no sadist, just a geek!) This is where you start looking at where and what you are spending. When I work with clients one to one and on my courses, we call this the

"Oh shit moment".

Why? Well you suddenly realise just how much you have been spending and wasting, and most people do look at me and say "Oh shit!!" I can guarantee you'll find that direct debit you forgot to cancel or that you're paying twice for. I've even had a client overpaying a loan for over four years, so you may find something similar and have a windfall refund! It's happened to me too – I found out I was paying for a well-known film subscription twice and hadn't noticed, so don't be surprised.

You need to go through each statement with a fine-toothed comb too; don't miss out a month or skip a page because you'll overlook something important and as I said, you only need to do this once or twice a year to check on yourself.

> *I'm sure you'll be rubbing your eyes, and my name will be mud, and you'll tell me you would rather stick pins in your eyes than do this process every year,*

but when you're running your business and paying yourself what you are worth, you'll thank me for this painful annual process. You may even find yourself so in touch with your inner financial geek, like me, you won't even have to repeat the process annually as no expenditure sneaks passed you unnoticed any more.

Cancel Everything Unnecessary

The next step once you've removed the pins from your eyes is to cancel anything you don't need. Check when direct debits or standing orders are due to finish and make a note. Ensure you keep this information for later on as we'll come back to this.

By now you will know where every penny of your money went over the last year and will probably kick yourself a little for some moments of irresponsible spending, but you've also been smiling at some of the good memories it has revived, so you see, it's not all bad!

Plot the Next 12 Months

Next, when you've cancelled the duplicate payments, categorised all your expenses and got past the weeping and wailing and "oh shit moments" etc., you are ready to start plotting out the next twelve months of your expenditure – no I'm not joking – I mean twelve whole months of your personal expenditure!

I want you to include any fun spends too, as it's not all about the bills and the ridiculous credit card debt you may need to face: if you're going into or are already in business, you need down-time and holidays too!

Most business coaches will tell you that before planning out your business year, plan in your holidays too. This makes sure you take some well-earned rests during the year, but you have got to pay for these too!

There may be periods in your business when, if you are not present, you do not earn.

> If so, you may feel me physically slap you now.

You'll learn why in the next chapter, so for now, sit with the slap.

Don't think about these right now, just plan out what you need every month. I don't encourage frivolity at this stage either as you need to be realistic. If you over-estimate your next twelve months' spending, it may be unachievable and you'll just start the downward spiral of thinking you have a poor business when actually, you don't, you may just have set your "Most Important Employee" salary too high at the beginning.

> Hopefully, by now you can see where this is all going, so you will be sat with your quill and parchment or your spreadsheet with your anticipated monthly salary.

It really is that simple! You should have a summary of all your monthly personal expenditure, from your morning coffee extravaganza to your rent or mortgage, from your weekly shop to your lovely holiday in the sun, all right there in front of you, every single penny you intend to spend over the next twelve months in black and white or red and green, whatever colour you have chosen to plot those all-important numbers.

That final total at the bottom of the page is your "Important Employee Salary"! This is the money you need every month to survive – the money you need your business to make to pay you at the end of each whole month of working your ass off.

So, instead of waving a finger in the air and stating to the world that you want to earn £100k or $100k a month and not being able to substantiate that number, now you know how much you really need to survive, to live on, to provide for your nearest and dearest, you've taken all the guesswork out of what salary you need. The icing on the cake is you are now in control of your personal finances too, your Personal Cashflow management. Your money won't manage you, you will manage your money and believe me, that is one powerful way to live!

> However... yeah I hate that word too... it's the big "but"... don't think it ends here just because you're gobbling down that icing on the cake; now you have to live and breathe it too and track it every day, week, month and year (back to sticking pins in your eyes).

Yes, I'm serious: whatever you do, don't forget to track your personal expenditure otherwise you'll be revisiting this chapter and wearing out the pages all too soon.

This is one big, no – HUGE lesson in business: ensuring you can pay you, and not ever forgetting that you need to pay "the Most Important Employee" in your business – YOU!

Recap:

1. Make sure you understand who is the Most Important Employee i.e. YOU, and keep this in your head at all times.

2. Build a Personal Cashflow in detail – remember, this is your salary.

3. There are no excuses for not paying yourself, if you get to this stage you've royally fucked up, so give me a call!

4. Track, track and track again.

Sally Brady

Chapter 8

The Financials Part Two: Financial Statements

Before we get started, let's dispel a couple of ridiculous myths:

"You need to be an Accountant or have an Accountant to understand the Financials of your business."

... and:

"You need to have a Degree, Masters, PHD, A Level, GCSE, O Level, CSE or any other bloody qualification in Maths to be successful in business"!

These two literally do my nut in, they are merely poor excuses for lazy business owners.

> The Financials of your business are KEY to your success.

If you choose to be lazy and let someone else take the reins, then you are not only lazy but a complete fool too.

I have seen businesses fail and businesses struggle because the owner used those excuses. You are not only the Most Important Employee in your business – you "OWN" the business, so take ownership and lead from the top by understanding every number within your business.

Accountants can be good for your business if you find a good one, but they can also assist in killing your business too. A lot are what they say on the tin: "Auditors or Accountants" and that's all they do. They are not business Coaches or Salespeople, they are Accountants who invariably know nothing about your business except what you may or may not tell them.

It just so happens they are trained in the Accounting laws of the land and principles that you are legally bound to follow.

If you haven't already gathered, this is a beef I have with business owners and Accountants alike.

I find that for some reason, business owners believe that all Accountants are good at what they do and trustworthy, so clients just hand over the reins of their business and walk away!!

Seriously, would you hand over your child or dog (just in case you don't have a child) to a random childminder or dogsitter, just because that's what they SAY they do, without checking them out first and making sure they are going to cherish your baby/kid/dog as much as you do? No, I didn't think so, so why oh why do it with your business?!?

I recently came across a business which had been paying an Accountant for over eight years for, not only the weekly bookkeeping and year-end Accounting, but for monthly meetings and business development and paying them A LOT of money.

The reality of the situation was the books were a mess, the owner had no idea of the true position of the business finances, monthly meetings were definitely not happening and, as for business development, well yes, that was a load of bullshit too.

> All this trust and no delivery.
> Even I was shocked at this one.

Another one I've had the pleasure of experiencing is the Accountant offering "Cashflow Management and Planning" as part of their service before the year-end each year. That, people, is not a good service offer!

A monthly planning and cash management service would be gold, but just before your year-end is not giving you good service. It is delivering one of two options:

- the bad news that you've had a bad year and have no money left in the bank so it's a rocky road ahead

- or you're about to hit a huge tax bill and you've got a month to run around like a lunatic and find some way of buying some capital item to benefit your business and avoid paying tax.

Accountants are good for completing your Year-End Accounts, auditing and tax compliance and that's it, the rest is down to you. It's all Management Information, commonly known as "MI", so this is why you need to get a grip of the Financials from Day One, and if you're already on your business journey and haven't grasped this yet, then get a grip now, it's not too late.

The best way to do this is to learn about the Financials or do some of the bookkeeping yourself for a while, even if you've already got a team around you doing the work. Have a go yourself, it's much easier than you think and it's invaluable what you'll learn.

You'll soon be challenging the numbers put in front of you each day/week/year and you'll definitely be challenging the grey-suit-brigade each year; never again will you accept those "year-end audit adjustments" so easily. This will open up a whole new world, a world where YOU CONTROL your money.

OK, so now I've had my rant, and hopefully you've listened, now we can really get into the nitty gritty of what Financials you need in your Business Plan.

The Profit & Loss

The Profit & Loss has a couple of pseudonyms. You may see it called the "Income and Expense Statement" or "Statement of Financial Results". It is a historic document in that it's produced after the end of a period in time, usually a month and/or a year, and it simply shows you what it says in the name, the income and the expenses of the business and the resulting profit or loss in that period.

It is not as many people think the same as the Cashflow Forecast or statement, the difference being that the numbers reported are usually net of any tax, so they don't include tax unless (and this is where you may roll your eyes) you cannot reclaim tax, then you need to enter gross figures and as I stated, it's "historic" so it's reporting on what has already happened within the business, whereas a Cashflow Forecast looks at the current situation using the bank account as the point of reference.

> *Whatever you like to call it, your Profit & Loss report will usually have a set format.*

I have templates available on my **Business Planning 101** course or check out my YouTube channel here: https://tinyurl.com/ye22k4dv.

First is income specifically relating to the business, then Direct Expenses – these are any costs directly associated with making a sale. Then it will give a total showing the Gross Profit, and then Administration Expenses, (also known as Overhead Expenses).

Next, it gives a total showing the Operating or Net Profit/Loss, then Dividends and Tax, and finally, the total Profit/Loss for the year, as shown below:

Profit & Loss
- Income (Sales)
- Less Direct Costs
- = Gross Profit
- Less Administration/Overhead Costs
- = Net/Operating Profit/Loss

- Less Dividends
- Less Tax
- = Total Profit/Loss

The area I see that causes most confusion is the difference in Direct Costs and Administration/ Overhead Costs, so here are some examples to make this clearer.

- Direct Expenses – these costs are specifically related to making a sale. If you are manufacturing a product, you may have employees who work on the product line, building or creating the product. They are a direct cost. Materials to make the product are direct costs too.

- Administration/Overhead costs – these costs are related to the overall running of the business, the rent of your office, stationery, salaries for you and your office staff, accountancy fees, legal fees and so on.

When creating the plan for a business, I always start from the bottom up as it's so much easier. Why? Because invariably you know the Fixed Costs of your business such as Rent and Rates, Consulting or Accountancy Fees, and Staff Salaries, so do the easy bit first. Plot out the known costs for twelve months to start with.

Once you have these numbers, this will drive your Sales and Direct Costs as the net of these two must cover your Administration/Overhead costs to enable you to make a Profit.

I'm not joking when I say this really focuses you on driving sales.

I had a client who was tracking her Profit & Loss and realised she was about to hit a blip, but by having the information in front of her, she knew if she made just one more sale of one of her three income streams, she could cover her overheads and bring the month back on track, and that is exactly what she did.

This also made her look closer at all the three income streams and realign her marketing focus as she realised this particular one was also the most profitable of the three!

Once you've bottomed out your known Fixed/Overhead costs, you will know exactly what you need to make in Gross Profit to cover the Overheads of the business, so now you can look at the sales: what is the Gross Profit of each of your income streams?

If you don't know this, now is the time to get to know this finer detail. Just for clarity, the Gross Profit (the Margin) is the Sale less any Direct Cost, as explained above.

So, look at making one of each Sale and what Gross Profit this will give you, then work out how many of each you need to sell each month to cover the total of your Fixed Costs – and bingo! You have your Sales and Direct Costs forecast!

> The clever bit in the Sales and Direct Costs forecast is the focus and drive from you as you don't want to just cover your overheads and break even, you want "PROFIT".

So push yourself, not to unreachable limits but enough to see a bigger impact each year and have growth.

I always say "Be sensible but not negative" here, as in my corporate days we were always set ridiculous targets that, in truth, we were never going to meet, and yes OK, it made us push a bit harder and deliver that bit more, but it was also a little soul destroying too. So work with a push, but a sensible one.

The Balance Sheet

This is the part that everyone thinks is complicated, and most business owners think it is beyond their brain power to understand – again,

> another complete and utter bullshit belief!

It is simply what it says on the tin: a "balancing sheet" balancing the Assets and Liabilities of your business with the Capital or Equity. It's just the terminology that scares you, another great lot of wordy phrases created by the grey-suit-brigade to justify their existence.

Assets come in two forms, Fixed and Current, and are things that you could realise or turn into cash to cover any debt (Liability) in the business.

Liabilities are again two types: the "current" ones are sometimes also referred to as "short term". Then you have the "long term", these are any monies the business owes.

Capital & Equity

Capital will be the amount you introduced into the business as a shareholder. Usually in smaller businesses you see this as the initial £1.00 or £100 you paid to set up the company. If you are a limited company, then the Equity is the profits or losses you are making year on year.

I am going to break down each term for you and then show you a diagram to help your understanding so that you'll no longer fear this mind-blowingly useful statement in your accounts.

Assets

Fixed Assets: Tangible and Intangible
Tangible – think about anything you can physically get your hands on, for example a chair, a vehicle, a piece of equipment you use to manufacture your product.

Intangible – this is something you cannot physically hold, so think about the goodwill you may have paid when you purchased the business. Many businesses don't have Intangible Assets but it's a good thing to know regardless.

Current Assets
If your bank account is healthy and in credit, it's a current asset. This might include prepayments for anything you have paid for in advance (such as a subscription to my **Business Planning 101** course that you could spread over six months) stock you are holding to manufacture your products, and Debtors The amounts your customers owe you.

Liabilities, Current or Short Term

Creditors
The amounts you owe your suppliers, your bank overdraft (as this could be recalled for payment within a short term)

Accruals
Accountants' fees you know you will have to pay so are saving money to pay the buggers. Think of accruals like saving for a holiday – you put the money away

each week or month and then draw the money out as you need it.

Taxes

You have to pay these usually within a month or year.

Liabilities, Long Term

Any bank loan you have taken over three years, hire purchase loans over three years, so basically, anything you have borrowed over a longer than three-year period.

Capital & Equity

Capital

Money that you or your shareholders have introduced into the business, the shareholding.

Equity

The profit or losses (we hope not) the business is making year on year, you usually see this stated as "retained profit/loss" and "current year profit/loss", so retained means the profit or losses made in previous years and current means the profit you made this year.

Balance Sheet

as of 31st December 2025

Assets

Current Assets

Cash	40,000
Accounts Receivable	70,000
Inventory	30,000
Total Current Assets	**140,000**

Long-term Assets

Machinery	5,000
Equipment	40,000
Total Long-term Assets	**45,000**

Total Assets	**£185,000**

Liabilities

Current Liabilities

Accounts Payable	30,000
Current Portion - Long-term Debt	20,000
Total Current Liabilities	**50,000**

Long-term Liabilities

Bank Loan	100,000
Total Long-term Liabilities	**100,000**

Total Liabilities	**£150,000**

Owner's Equity

Owner's Capital	25,000
Returned Earnings	10,000
Total Owner's Equity	**35,000**

Total Liabilities + Owner's Equity	**£150,000**

Hopefully this has made the Balance Sheet much clearer for you, so that you can now build your own. It's not difficult. As with everything, it's about the knowledge.

> One thing I must share with you is please, please, please keep your Balance Sheet in a positive state.

What I mean is that your Assets need to remain higher than your Liabilities. If the balance goes into negative, this is not good – it means you are literally borrowing beyond your means, and you don't have the Assets to cover your debts! So, when looking at your Balance Sheet each month, look at how you are trading, you need to be trading in PROFIT.

If you are looking to borrow, then a bank or lender will look at your ability to repay, and this involves looking at your Balance Sheet. The big mistake I see is the business owner who constantly pays dividends to themselves with no regard to whether or not they are making a profit.

> Don't do it! This just makes you a Creditor or a Liability of your business!

I have seen a business owner turned down by several lenders due to being a Liability of their business. Not only is it poor business management, it also means you have to pay it back or else be subject to a big fat personal tax bill.

Last but not least, measure both of these statements. Set yourself some "KPI's" – key performance indicators. Here's another fancy name but don't overthink these either.

Think about setting yourself a target such as the percentage gross and net profit you want to make each month and year, and maybe look at keeping your Debtors and Creditors at a certain level; nothing fancy, just some good measures to keep you on track.

You need to see clearly where you are going and if you are meeting your goal. This important step is one to keep checking in with regularly, preferably monthly.

Recap:

1. You don't need a grey suit or to be a master at Maths to understand the Financials of your business.

2. Create a Profit & Loss Statement for your business, build it from the bottom up, challenge yourself with your sales forecast but be realistic.

3. The Balance Sheet – no bullshit here; it's simple to understand, and the aim is to keep it positive. Negatives are a no-go area, so if they can be avoided, avoid them.

4. Measure, measure and measure again. Create some simple measures to keep you on track with both your Profit and Loss and the Balance Sheet and make sure you track them monthly.

Chapter 9

The Financials
Part Three:
The Business Cashflow

Cashflow is absolutely the **KING or QUEEN** within your business. Master this little beauty and you'll smash the business controls right out of the water.

However, it's the one I always find gets missed out in businesses. Why, oh why should I??? I hear you ask. Well, it's something I say way too often: it's the **ULTIMATE** way of controlling the business finances, yet it gets left out all the time.

A couple of years ago, I went to see the owner of a very successful business: a multi-million pound turnover and making good profits. We had a lovely conversation, and at the end of that meeting he said, "Great to get to know you, but we don't need your services right now, but stay in touch." I shook his hand and said "See you in a few months," and he laughed.

But you see, during that meeting I had asked lots of questions, keen to know about the business and its successes, and understand how they managed their finances etc. Life and business are always a learning curve, and I'm that nosey person who likes to know all about you and your business, as I'm still learning too, in fact we all are.

The information I gained during that meeting was that, whilst they were apparently making lots of profit and had millions in the bank, they actually had no cash forecasting in place; they were using the "Bank Checking Method".

In other words, they had no visibility of their cash position, they were merely relying on the fact they had around a million in the bank and assumed that was enough to ensure stability, so each week they were checking the bank balance and saying to themselves, "Yep we're OK, and we can pay all the wages, suppliers, dividends and still have lots of dosh left over."

> WRONG, absolutely bloody WRONG, if you run a business purely on the "Bank Checking Method", you are heading straight off the cliff and need a damn good slap!

What you are not doing is ensuring your Debtors and Customers are paying on time, that you are being efficient in paying your Creditors, that you have enough should that big fat client not pay, that you have enough for the next few months or years should we hit another global pandemic or other crisis. You are basically running your business BLIND, with not a damn clue of how your finances look now or in the future.

> If this is you, stop now, just stop right now and make sure you read on or contact me as this is an EMERGENCY!

Anyway, on with my story. As you can probably guess, within a couple of months I received a phone call requesting a meeting, as "We think you can help us. Our cash has depleted significantly and we're not sure why." No, I wasn't smug at all, not my way, although we do laugh about it now and I can be smug as they are in a much different place.

The one thing I did immediately, before even starting on Cost Reviews and Debtor/Customer payments was to get a Cashflow Report in place. We needed to understand where the cash was being haemorrhaged or why there was not enough coming in to cover their costs. Mapping the Cashflow and plotting the next few months showed me exactly what was happening, so we could then manage the situation.

> None of this is beyond you and yes, I may be that smart-arsed eagle-eyed cash tracker, but that doesn't mean you can't be too.

Like everything else I have shown you so far in this book, cash forecasting is not this magical thing that only financy geeks can do. It is simple and is perhaps the key essential in helping you manage the finances of your business.

I have some very simple templates you can use, and even a few videos on YouTube you can watch to help you after reading this chapter and the next. Yep, two whole chapters dedicated to Cashflow Forecasting, it's that important!

An interesting question I have been asked a lot is,

> "Do I still need to run and monitor my Cashflow Forecast when I'm successful?"

Now, there are two things I would say here, the first is, "As this measure is different for us all, at what point do you see yourself as successful?" and secondly, "Yep absolutely, as what you have today may be gone tomorrow if you don't keep your eye on the ball," just like my millionaire company described above. So my answer in a nutshell is,

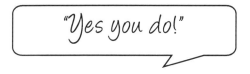

"Yes you do!"

OK, so let's look more into why you need this pesky report that you currently hate the thought of but will eventually love with all your heart:

1. It gives you visibility to ensure you can pay your bills and expenses, your wages, your rent or business mortgage, your factory or office running costs.

2. It gives you the visibility to see when you can invest in growth, such as new equipment to break into a new market, or simply manufacture more products more efficiently.

3. It gives you visibility so that you can prepare for the unexpected, such as a dirty little pandemic that would wipe other companies out.

4. It gives investors visibility as to whether you are a viable investment. If you're managing your cash then you will have a healthy Cashflow, so you are a good investment.

So, are you seeing the constant factor in all four of the above? Yep you got it:

"Visibility"

The Cashflow is all about giving you visibility, the visibility to make clear and informed decisions about your business, and as a geek would say, "Having a positive Cashflow is essential for your business's survival and growth and financial stability."

Many business owners confuse the Profit and Loss and the Cashflow Reporting and tend to lump them together. To be fair, they can look very similar, but they are very different in terms of the information they actually give you, and whilst yes, they do feed each other, they are two very different animals.

Yep, you guessed it right again, I'm about to help you understand the difference between the Profit and Loss and the Cashflow Reporting.

I did touch on this in Chapter 8, but it's good to get your head back in the game and give you more of an insight and, trust me (she says as her devil horns rise out of her head), this is useful information and will help you build the Cashflow Report/Forecast.

I've no doubt when you start, questions will arise about the differences as they always do, so having a good understanding from the start helps. I'm not just saying it to fill another page in this book to kill my writer's cramp!

OK, Let's Cover the Profit and Loss First.

This, simply put, is a historic statement that covers all the company's revenue and expenses, including depreciation and amortisation and shows the net income of the business over a specific period of time. Right – now I'll put that into plain English for us human folk.

"Historic" means that the time or period that the Profit and Loss covers has already happened, it's history. Yes, of course you use a Profit and Loss Forecast for building your future Business Plan, but here I am covering the differences between the two reports, so when you are reporting Profit or Loss, this has already happened.

Usually you would produce your Profit and Loss as part of monthly management reporting information after the month or year has finished, so you can look back and review how the business performed during that period.

The Profit and Loss covers your income and expenses, all without tax, so "net of tax" – you do not include any tax that has been added to your sales or expenses. This is posted to the Balance Sheet so that you have a record of what to pay the lovely taxman later in the month or year. So all figures are excluding tax.

For Profit and Loss purposes, you are not interested in the tax as it's not your money; the tax you charge on your sales belongs to the HMRC or IRS, and the tax you pay on your business expenses forms part of the deduction of sales tax you pay, so again, this is not your money.

All tax belongs to the State, not you, so you don't need to report this in your Profit and Loss. The only tax you report on your Profit and Loss Report is the tax you will be required to pay for making a profit, so this is shown as per the diagram in Chapter 8 after the "Net/ Operating Profit/Loss".

Next Up is Depreciation and Amortisation

Again, these are the workings between the Balance Sheet and Profit and Loss. They are a way of expensing the Capital Assets you have acquired within the business, so you report these on the Profit and Loss only, as they are in reality "adjustments", they are not cash items. The initial purchase of the asset is the cash outlay and that goes onto the Balance Sheet.

Finally for the Profit and Loss, you are showing the net income or loss over a period of time. This profit is generating the cash for the business, so if you are making a profit, you are generating cash you could reinvest and you have a healthy Cashflow. If you are making losses, then you are not generating any cash for the business.

However, if you have previously made a profit, being in a loss at year-end does not necessarily mean all is bad as, if you have made a profit in previous months, you may have enough cash to cover the fact you have made a loss.

On to the Cashflow

The Cashflow is what I personally describe as the "here and now". It is reporting and looking at what you currently have in the bank and can physically get your hands on, so the money has already been deposited by the sales you have created or the money you have invested. It's real, you could physically touch it if you withdrew it all from the bank right now, so real-time information.

When you are reporting Cashflow, you include all sales and expenses as gross, so including tax. We are now looking at the money you have received into the bank, i.e. the total bank credit or deposit from a customer. The amount they will pay you is the whole amount, including any tax you charged on behalf of our lovely tax authorities. Then you show all the expenses you paid which will include tax as your suppliers have charged you tax too.

Tax

There is a line for this in your Cashflow as once a month, quarter or year, you may owe sales taxes, (VAT or Corporation Tax or some form of business tax) to your government treasury, so you need to put down the amount you will physically pay them, and this money will come out of your bank account, as you have collected the money on their behalf or made a profit for which you have to pay tax.

You do not include depreciation or amortisation as these are not items or expenses you pay monthly or yearly. What you would include would be the actual purchase of the asset – the equipment or laptop or whatever, as you physically part with the money and you hand it over to the supplier.

Or in the case of amortisation, if you purchased another company and you paid the owner a figure for his goodwill, you would put the amount in your Cashflow, if you physically hand this over.

Finally, the Cashflow Report

You are recording the actual cash received and expenses paid out of your business bank account, including any loan payments, tax payments, dividends you may pay yourself (assuming you are profitable of course), so any actual flow of cash in or out of your business.

Hopefully, you now have a better understanding of the difference between the Profit and Loss and the Cashflow:

> one is <u>historic</u> and one is here and now. The items you record are similar, but one is net of tax and one is gross (including tax).

As I mentioned earlier in the chapter, it is important to really get a good understanding of this. In the next chapter, I am going to talk you through building a Cashflow Forecast as this is such a milestone in business to enable you to easily manage and control your finances.

Each chapter in this book gives you all the key elements to building a Business Plan to help you grow your business and make a sustainable profit, and this one is the most important of all, so get it right. If you are already in business and not tracking your cash, now is the time to start, it will make a huge difference to your Business Planning.

Recap:

1. Cashflow is King or Queen in your business. Take time to master the report and understand it fully.

2. Only you can measure your success, but never stop tracking your cash.

3. Understand the difference between a Profit and Loss and a Cashflow Report.

4. Start building your Cashflow today – don't delay, it will cost you in the long term.

Sally Brady

Chapter 10

The Financials Part Four: Building The Business Cashflow

In Chapter 9, I have talked you through why you need a Cashflow, the difference between the Profit and Loss and a Cashflow Report/Forecast. Now we need to get right into the nitty-gritty of building the initial Cashflow and the Forecast.

To make things easier, I am going to actually focus on the Cashflow Forecast as this is what you ultimately need for your Business Planning.

Before we start, I need to issue the following warning:

> Do not, I repeat DO NOT let anyone tell you that you cannot create a Cash Forecast for twelve months or beyond or just to use your Accounting software.

> They are probably a "grey suit" or a person lacking significant knowledge, so send them my way.

If this were true, I simply would not be in business today!

Now, on with the task in hand. The Cashflow Report is your actual starting point and the forecasting is, as it states, the forecast or view for the future cash of the business. If you are already in business, make a start using the actual date of your last month of business and that end balance. If you are new to business and have not started yet, then you are literally starting from zero.

Do not cheat yourself by missing things out; only you will pay when you fall on your face. On the other hand, don't be so optimistic it's unachievable, just be realistic and don't overthink what you are about to create and do. We have no room or time for procrastination here. The reason I say don't overthink or procrastinate is that we will review it at the end, it's better just to get the data in and get this thing built.

I have a series of YouTube videos on how to build a Cashflow Forecast in 5 days, and no, it doesn't take five full days, it's just a series of 5 videos, one per day. You set aside one hour per day to complete each of the steps I am about to take you through in this chapter, so there's additional help for you in listening to my lovely northern tones talking you through this, as well as reading it on paper. https://tinyurl.com/ye22k4dv

The next steps are very similar to the Personal Cashflow I talked about in Chapter 7. In fact so similar I actually run my Personal Cashflow and Business Cashflow in the same spreadsheet, not only based on their similarities but the fact that the two are interlinked, so this is where you need to have your Personal Cashflow at the ready so you can input the information you built earlier too.

First step of course is to pick your tool of choice (or poison as the mini-me likes to say.) For the business Cashflow, I don't suggest you use the quill and parchment or pen and paper: here it is much more useful to use a spreadsheet of any particular brand of your choosing, but as we are talking business, you will need to easily update, track and manipulate this forecast daily, weekly, monthly and yearly, so choose something simple and that works for you. Just to repeat my comments in Chapter 7,

> *I'd advise you to stay away from the cash modelling and forecasting software at this point as I have yet to find one that is as smart and manipulative as the human brain.*

Once you are ready, we can begin. Yep, I love a story time! Ha, all joking aside, it's time to start planning the Cash Forecast. If you have already started in business, then you need to grab your bank statement from the last month as we are going to use the information in there to start to build the first month. If you are new to business, then read on as this will help you too.

Start by marking out 12 months in columns on your sheet. In the rows, you want the top to be **Income**, then a sub-total for all the income lines. Following that, you have **Expenses** with lots of lines below so you can list the expense categories you need, then another sub-total to total the expenses.

Below this, a formula for
Income – Expenses = Net Income/Expenses.
Finally another row for your bank balance, then the sum of the *Bank Balance – Net Income/Expenses*.

It should look like the following example:

Cash Forecast

	Jan	Feb	Mar	Apr
Income:				
Sales				
Non-Widget Sales				
Miscellaneous	-	-		
Total Income	-	-	-	-
Expenditure:				
Cost of Sales				
Delivery Costs				
IT Software/Subscriptions				
Mobile Phone				
Telephone/Internet				
Insurance				
Car Insurance				
Social Media				
Storage				
Office				
Wages				
Directors Wages/Renumeration				
Pension				
Tax to transfer to savings				
Total Expenditure	-	-	-	-
Net income/(outflow):	-	-	-	-
Bank Balance B/fwd	2,000.00	2,000.00	2,000.00	2,000.00
Balance C/fwd	**2,000.00**	**2,000.00**	**2,000.00**	**2,000.00**

I do have templates you can use if you need one, so don't feel you have to reinvent the wheel, just give me a shout and tell me you're on Chapter 10 of my book and can you please have a template and I'll happily send you one.

As I stated earlier in the book, I always start from the bottom and work up, working arse-about-face, so we are going to look at costs first as they are easier to plot. So with your last month's bank statement, go through and find all the "fixed" costs – anything you pay regularly. It should be relatively easy if you pay via Direct Debit.

Put these costs in the first month against their categories, so for example if you use particular software packages, do as I have done above and create a header in one of the rows for *"IT/Software/ Subscriptions",* then on to the next cost and do the same until you have covered all your known costs.

If you don't have any history and are just starting out, then simply list out what you think you will need, and either research the cost of use or an approximate cost that is realistic. You will be tracking this later on, so will start learning the true costs and can update as you go.

Once you have all your known costs in, add them into the following twelve months' columns. If you know they are going to increase or decrease in a particular month, then make sure you factor this in; if you have costs that happen bi-monthly, quarterly, or annually, make sure you put these into the relevant months.

If you have wages or salaries to pay that are fixed or remain roughly the same, make sure you factor these in too – and don't forget the one Fixed cost which is extremely important that needs to go in, that is paying the most Important Employee of the Business... YOU!

This is where your Personal Cashflow from Chapter 7 comes into play: you need to have a single line just for you, your wages, what you will be drawing out of the business to survive and live your life.

Once you have all your Fixed Costs in, we can move on to the Sales and unknown/Variable Costs and Taxes and this is where your knowledge kicks in.

Sales first. Again, if you are already in business, in the first column, (using last month's data), put in the amount in total, including tax you received in the last month. Then go to your outstanding Invoice/Debtors list and plot over the next few months when you expect to collect the remaining amounts.

Then it's time to get smart: what do you expect to receive in Sales in the next twelve months? What do you want to generate in sales turnover month-on-month in your business? Then think over the last month's sales: how do your customers pay? Did they pay within 7, 10 or 30 days and beyond? Plot this information.

I usually insert three or four rows showing the sales split into how customers pay, so I would say 60% of my turnover (another word for income) is paid in 7 days, so that goes in the first row. The remaining 30% is paid over 10 or 30 days, so I have a row for each of those. This does get easier as you track: you will start to see patterns in your sales turnover and how people pay you, and it will certainly focus you on getting your invoices paid on time.

Once you have plotted your sales, you then move on to the variable costs/cost of sales. These are the amounts that change monthly depending on your sales. If you are like me, then lucky you, you may only have a few or none at all of these types of costs, but if you are making a product then you will, of course, have costs for making that product which will vary depending on your sales, so this is where you need to know your cost of sales and the delivery of those sales.

If you have not worked out your cost of sales, the cost of making your product, distributing your product or the cost of your service, do this now. Simply calculate every item that is associated with making one sale.

Do not include the Fixed Costs such as computer software, telephones, office costs etc. as these costs do not change whether you make one sale or a hundred sales – this is simply the costs of making an item. Then multiply this by the number of sales you are going to make each month of this particular item. Do this for each of your sales lines/income streams.

When plotting the costs of sales each month, make sure you factor in any changes in the UK economy and price increases. I know this is not easy but try and do this from a reasonable perspective. Again, you will be revisiting this so you can make changes as you learn.

Factor in the costs of delivering your product too: how much is postage or courier service for each sale? Once again, these are costs that vary when making a sale, so you have to use your sales plan here to make your costs as accurate as possible.

Finally, on to the tax. If you are registered for paying tax on sales and recouping tax on your purchases (in the UK it's VAT) then work out the tax amount on all the sales you make each month, and then deduct anything you can reclaim.

I would strongly advise that you put this amount into your Cashflow Forecast and then move that money to a savings account each month so that you always have your tax money ready to pay.

> Yep you guessed it: again, this is something I see all the time, people not planning the tax into their cash forecasting, but not having the money to pay the lovely taxman is not a good position to be in!

So at the end of this you should have your Sales, Variable Costs, Cost of Sales, Fixed Costs/Overheads and your Taxes all plotted out over the next twelve months. Now how easy was that?

A Cashflow by magic... now the tricky part.

Look back over everything you have done and see the results. You may be way off reality but you do have all the information in front of you to start reviewing and making it real. You may have already done this as you have worked on each month. Personally I plot everything out first to see where I land and then start to really work on it, it's easier when you have the whole year in front of you.

At this point you may look and see that your costs are really heavy and therefore question the figure you have in sales income. Is this reasonable? Could you do more each month to generate more cash? Or are your costs too high, and you've been too pessimistic?

So go back and review your costs. You may find you are a genius, and you have everything looking all rosy. Either way this will not be perfect. This is the guide for you, and as you track each month, this gets better and better and you become more and more accurate as you learn more about the money flows within your business.

This is when you start to manage your money and it stops managing you, or again, if you are new to business, then this is where you can start on a good path, and you manage your money from Day One.

It's empowering and gives you so much visibility to grow and sustain your business. If you were around in the pandemic you will know how devastating that was for businesses, but now, by having this information about your future sales and costs, you would be able to see what is ahead of you to plan to survive.

> As you get smarter with this, you will cope with any shit that the world throws at you from a monetary perspective so, please, please, please don't drop the ball on this one

make sure you track it daily, weekly, monthly and yearly. Build out the next 2-3 years too and measure. Make this your main KPI and make me proud of you!

Recap:

1. Choose a tool that works for you, and you can easily work with.

2. Start from the bottom up and plot the known costs first.

3. Make your sales predictions realistic but push yourself, don't be unrealistic.

4. Don't forget the Most Important Employee in the business

5. Make a line in your Cash Forecast for your Taxes and make sure you save for them; they are a necessary evil.

6. This won't be perfect, but you'll get smarter every day.

7. TRACK TRACK TRACK!

Chapter 11

Terminology and Jargon

Bullshit – the general term for wafflers who spout unnecessary shit

BP101 – A damn good course you should join

Grey Suit – Accountant

Pivot – a bollocks term born out from idiots during Covid-19

Fail – something you won't do if you read this book and plan

Business Plan – the documented map of the goals of your business

Dogshit – the smell of a desperate sale

Business Owner – YOU

Tax – a necessary evil and the result of profit

Work life Balance – a myth it doesn't exist, be smart and you can live life to the full

Dividend – only payable when you are profitable, it's not a monthly wage

Most important employee – YOU

Profit & Loss – historic statement showing the profitability or losses of your business.

Balance Sheet – the historic statement that balances your Assets and Liabilities

Cashflow – The King or Queen of your business

Bank Checking Method – a methodology giving you no visibility of the cash position of your business

Success – Something only you can measure

Arse about face – how I build forecasting models

Smart Business Owner – one who plans and forecasts and tracks and makes a profit

Sustainable Profit – something you can achieve if you plan

Business Growth – attainable via planning and forecasting

Dropping the ball – not tracking and measuring your forecasts and plans

Perfect – something that doesn't exist. You'll learn, grow, and adapt your plans

Chapter 12

The End

Well, hopefully you've read this far in the book and now have a clear plan, or process for your plan, and have enjoyed at least some of my wit and humour.

When I say I'm interested in your journey, I truly am; I like to hear all about successes and if you need help then shout. As I have said so many times, I have a damn good Business Planning Course you can join, or maybe you want to work with me on a 1:1 basis. Anyway these are all choices open to you.

The journey for me has been about documenting everything I do in my own business and will continue to do. As I have said in the main content of the book, every day we are learning, and every day is a school day. My aim has been to show you how easy this can be, and it's not all about being a genius in business or at Maths.

The best advice I can give you is this: if you are starting in business, start off on the right foot and have a decent plan that maps your journey. Don't fall foul to the wing and a prayer and "I don't have time for this" scenario. Do it the right way and you'll have a much better journey. Be clear on who you are and where you want to go.

Those of you who have already started, or been in business for a while, it's not too late to change your dirty habits. You can create a plan for your future, or for your exit or sale, or simply just to have the true visibility you need. It's not good to be working with no future end-goal mapped. It's messy so it's time to tidy up.

I really need to crack on now as I have planning and tracking to do; this business waits for no man, so here's to a planned retirement in twenty years where I can be more annoying and tell the grandkids what a whizz I was at this business shit.

> Have fun planning and say "Hi" along the way!

Don't forget you can find out if you are ready to plan for profit, here: https://tinyurl.com/2p87nvcx.

https://sallybrady.co.uk/

sally@sallybrady.co.uk

in https://www.linkedin.com/in/sallybrady-businessplanningspecialist

About the Author

I worked as a successful Accountant and Senior Manager in the Corporate Sector for over 30 years, I understand and have experienced life when profit margins and people are squeezed and the overwhelming pressure this brings. Having my own company, I am fully aware of the struggles of the business owner and the many hats we have to wear and how planning is imperative within Business.

I spent so long in the Corporate sector and saw so many great leaders with so very little knowledge of financials, but with a strong team behind them to support and grow the business, something your average SME does not have.

SME's have to have a hands-on approach to most aspects of their business and the Financials are the part most find so difficult and therefore bury their heads in the sand around this area. I see this as a key driver and want to ensure that SME's have this vital knowledge to help them grow and succeed in a highly competitive world.

I have successfully turned struggling Businesses with excessive losses into profit with continuous and sustainable growth, within 4 months turning a 140% Net Loss into a 40% Net Profit. My gift is Finances, give me any failing business and I can tell you where they're going wrong and how to fix it.

Printed in Great Britain
by Amazon

23137755R00077